Further Reading

Fighter Aircraft Facts for Kids
https://kids.kiddle.co/Fighter_aircraft

History of Flight
https://www.grc.nasa.gov/www/k-12/UEET
/StudentSite/historyofflight.html

Murray, Aaron R. *Modern Military Aircraft.* New York: PowerKids, 2016.

Murray, Laura K. *Fighter Jets.* Mankato, MN: Creative Education, 2016.

Nagelhout, Ryan. *Fighter Planes.* New York: Gareth Stevens, 2015.

Index

Photo Acknowledgments

Image credits: US Marine Corps photo by Cpl. Rachel E. Conrad, p. 2; US Navy photo, p. 4; U.S. Air Force photo by Senior Airman Kaylee Dubo, p. 5; US Air Force photo by Staff Sgt. Carlin Leslie, pp. 6, 7; Wikimedia Commons (public domain), p. 8; Library of Congress (LC-USZ62-106324), p. 9; National Archives (342-FH-3A42096), p. 10; US Air Force photo by Senior Airman Erin Trower, p. 11; US Air Force photo by Todd Cromar, p. 12; US Army photo by Staff Sgt. Austin Berner, p. 13; US Air Force photo by Samuel King Jr., p. 14; Rob Shenk/ Wikimedia Commons (CC BY-SA 2.0), p. 15; US Air Force photo by Tech. Sgt. Michael R. Holzworth, p. 16; US Air Force photo by Master Sgt. Michael Jackson, p. 17; US Air Force photo by Senior Airman Damon Kasberg, p. 18; jon666/iStock/Getty Images, p. 19; US Air Force photo by Justin Connaher, p. 20; US Air Force photo by Jamal Wilson, p. 22.

Cover: US Air Force photo by Staff Sgt. Jacob N. Bailey.

Main body text set in Billy Infant regular 28/36. Typeface provided by SparkType.

How Fighter Jets Work

Candice Ransom

Lerner Publications ◆ Minneapolis

LIGHTNING BOLT BOOKS™

Lerner Publications Company
An imprint of Lerner Publishing Group, Inc.
241 First Avenue North
Minneapolis, MN 55401 USA

For reading levels and more information, look up this title at www.lernerbooks.com.

Library of Congress Cataloging-in-Publication Data

Names: Ransom, Candice F., 1952- author.
Title: How fighter jets work / Candice Ransom.
Description: Minneapolis : Lerner Publications, [2020] | Series: Lightning bolt books. Military machines | Audience: Age 6-9. | Audience: K to Grade 3. | Includes bibliographical references and index.
Identifiers: LCCN 2018046429 (print) | LCCN 2018047234 (ebook) | ISBN 9781541556591 (eb pdf) | ISBN 9781541555693 (lb : alk. paper)
Subjects: LCSH: Fighter planes—Juvenile literature.
Classification: LCC UG1242.F5 (ebook) | LCC UG1242.F5 R346 2020 (print) | DDC 358.4/383—dc23

LC record available at https://lccn.loc.gov/2018046429

Manufactured in the United States of America
1-46024-43347-2/25/2019

Table of Contents

Fast Fighter Jets

A fighter jet zooms above desert sands. A loud boom follows the jet's burst of speed. The plane is flying faster than the speed of sound!

The pilot punches the jet's nose cone through the clouds. The aircraft cruises at 768 miles (1,236 km) per hour. Soon the jet will be back in the United States.

This is the jet's nose cone.

Fighter jets are military aircraft. Jets transport weapons and attack enemy planes.

The pilot's mission was a test. She flew over enemy lands. Enemy radar did not spot the jet.

The History of Fighter Jets

In 1903, Wilbur and Orville Wright invented the first airplane. The US military wanted to use planes for war. In 1909, the first Wright Military Flyer was built.

The first military planes usually carried one or two people.

Military airplanes first flew during World War I (1914–1918). The heavy wooden planes had two sets of wings. Pilots flew over camps and spied on their enemies.

Fighter planes fly with a bigger bomber plane to protect it.

By World War II (1939–1945), US fighter planes were made of metal. They could fly 425 miles (684 km) per hour.

Later fighter planes used radar to find enemy vehicles. Jet engines made the planes faster. Special materials made the jets lighter.

A group of fighter jets soars through the sky.

Parts of a Fighter Jet

Most fighter jets have a crew of one, the pilot. She sits in the cockpit. The pilot steers and controls the speed of the fighter jet.

Parachutes can be used to deliver supplies and soldiers to battle.

In an emergency, the pilot's seat lifts him out of the jet. A parachute opens so he can land safely.

Two powerful engines allow the jet to fly faster than the speed of sound. Weapons are under the wings and inside the plane.

This jet has missiles under its wings.

The jet is more than 62 feet (19 m) long. Most of the jet's surfaces are curved. Curved shapes make the jet hard to spot with radar.

Fighter Jets in Action

Modern fighter jets can be in the air in minutes. They can fly 1,500 miles (2,414 km) per hour. That is almost twice the speed of sound!

A fighter jet launches a missile from high in the sky.

In battles, fighter jets use their guns and fire missiles. Some missiles hit objects in the air, such as enemy planes.

A member of the military loads a jet's missiles.

Other missiles strike objects on land. This helps protect military troops that are on the ground.

In the future, fighter jets might not have pilots. People on the ground may fly the jets with remote controls.

The US military is always designing new fighter jets to use on missions.

Fighter Jet Diagram

cockpit

wings

tail

nose cone

body

engines

Fighter Jet Facts

- The United States Air Force, Navy, and Marines all use fighter jets. The air force has the most fighter aircraft.

- Some fighter jets are painted in colors and patterns that make them hard to see against different backgrounds. Planes flying over deserts are tan and brown. Jets flying over forests are many shades of green.

- The newest jets have no switches or dials. They have touch-screen controls, like a tablet computer.

Glossary

cockpit: a cabin in an aircraft where the pilot sits

cruise: to travel at the best operating speed

missile: a weapon that can strike a distant object

nose cone: the front, pointed part of an aircraft

parachute: a device that lets someone safely jump from an aircraft

radar: a device that sends radio waves to locate an object